BUDDY GUY

GUITAR ANTHOLOGY SERIES

Project Manager: Jeannette DeLisa
Music Editor: Aaron Stang
Art Design: Joseph Klucar

BLACK NIGHT

Words and Music by
JESSIE MAE ROBINSON

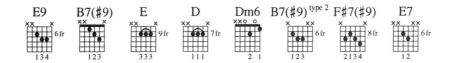

*When "A" is bent, the G string bends
automatically producing the F to F♯ bend.

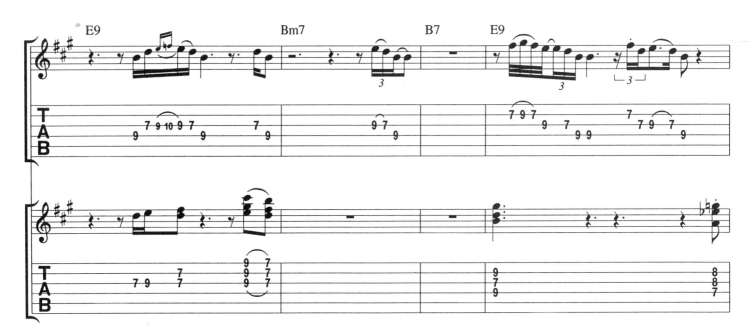

4

§ *Verse:*
w/Fill 3 *(Gtr. 1) 2nd & 3rd time*
w/Fill 2 *(Gtr. 2) 2nd time*
B7(♯9)

w/Fill 3 *(Gtr. 1) 3rd time*
E9

Gtr. 2

Black night is fall - in'. ___
I have no one to talk with, ___
Oh how I hate to be ___
to tell my trou-ble to. ___
a - lone.

B7(♯9)

My ba - by gone and left me. Some-one tell me what more, what more can I do.
My broth-er's in I-raq, and I don't know, I don't know what to do.

let ring

*one finger bends both the A and the F♮ simultaneously

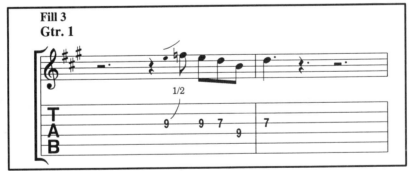

Fill 3
Gtr. 1

Fill 2
Gtr. 2

Black Night – 10 – 3

and there is an-oth-er day ___ is gone. ___

Guitar Solo:

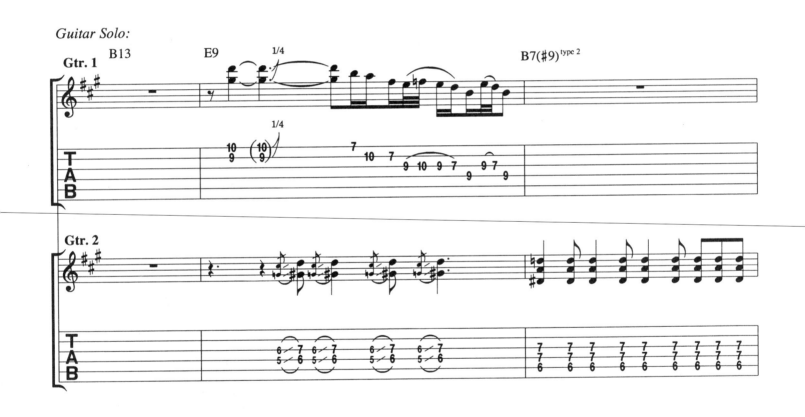

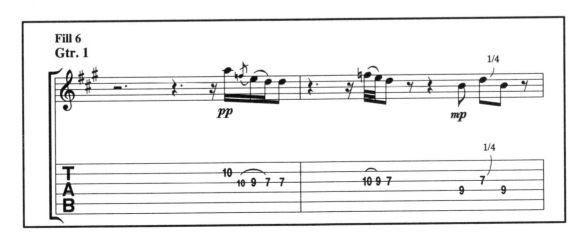

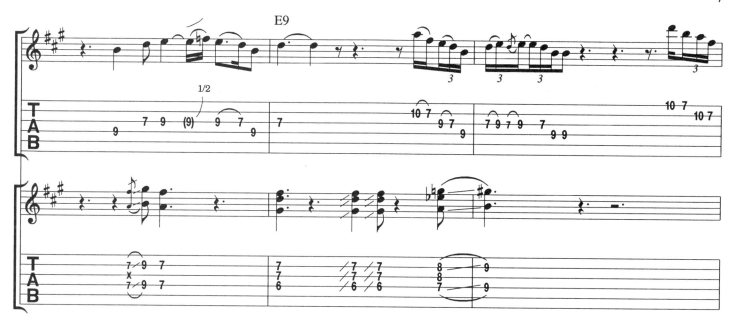

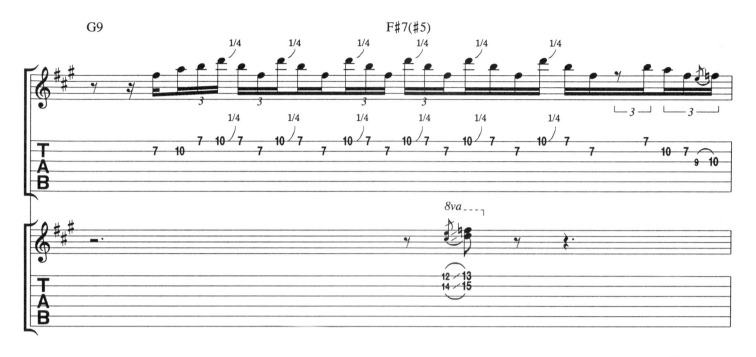

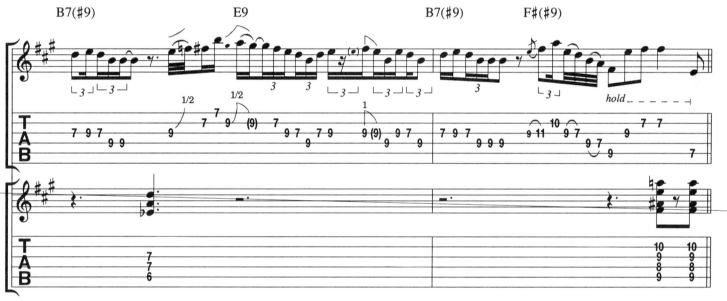

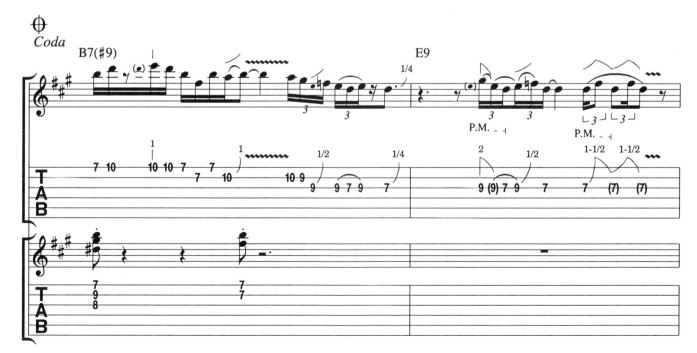

*Bend is executed by pulling the
string, not pushing.

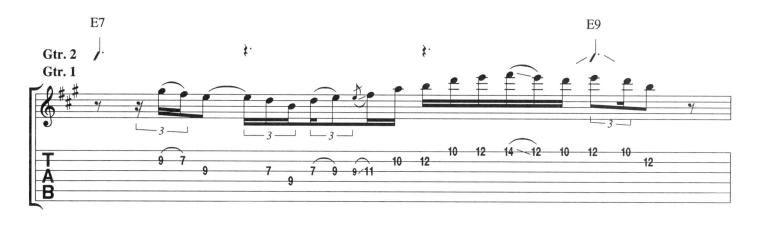

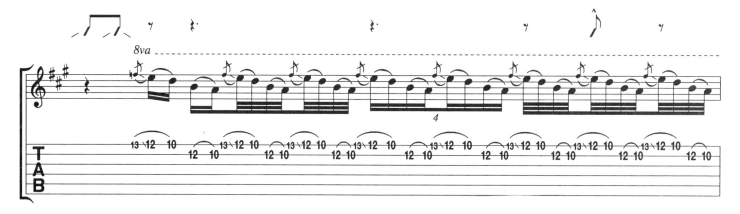

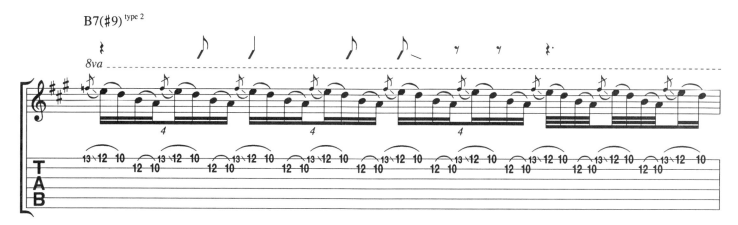

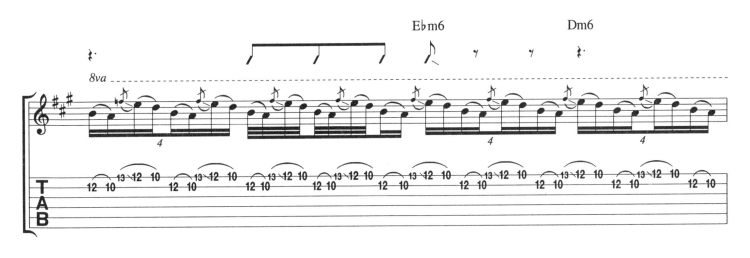

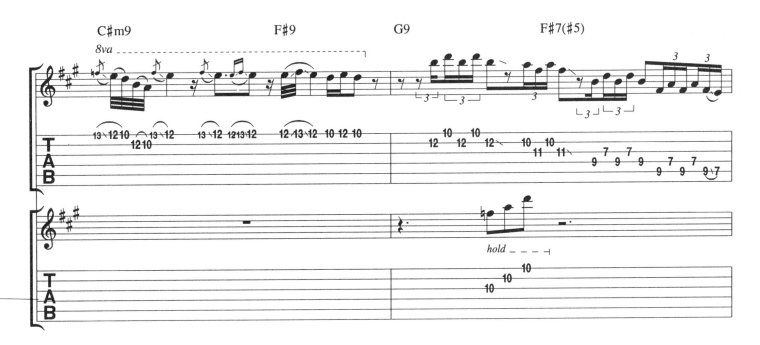

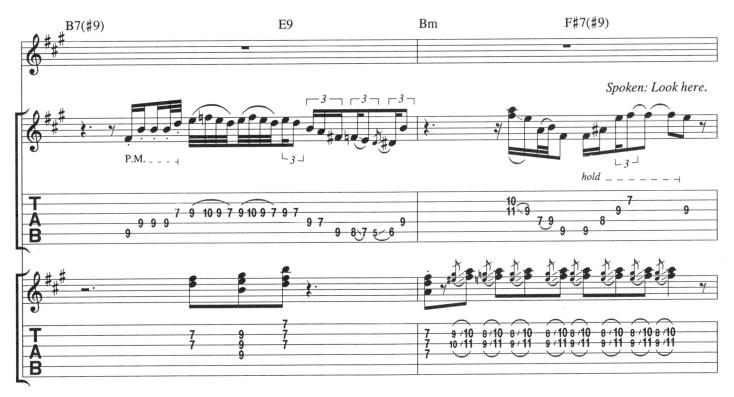

CHANGE IN THE WEATHER

Words and Music by
J. C. FOGERTY

Verse:
C7

ah, huh, you bet-ter duck and run.___

2.3. *See additional lyrics*

end Solo

last time only

Am

w/Fill 1 *(last time)*
F

Get un-der cov-er 'cause a change has come.___

(2nd time only)

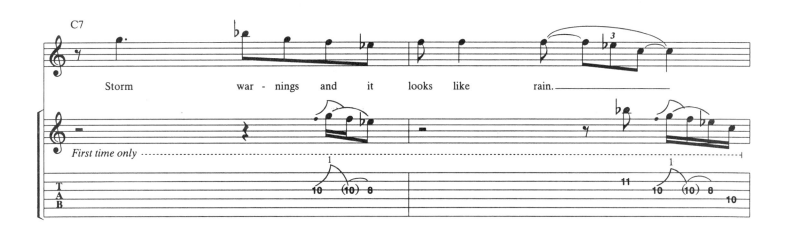

C7

Storm war-nings and it looks like rain.___

First time only

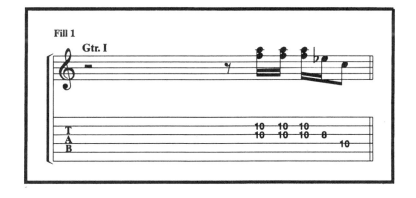

Fill 1
Gtr. I

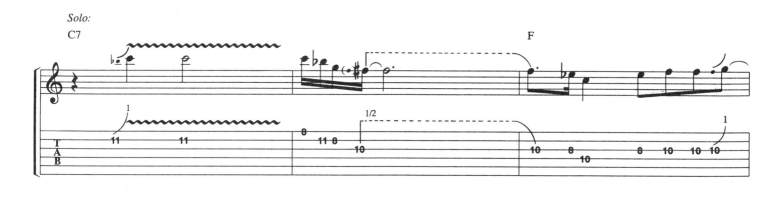

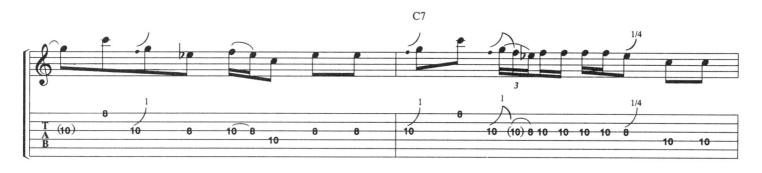

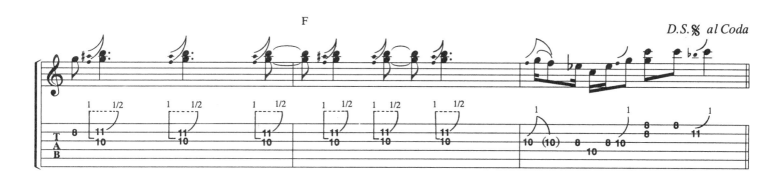

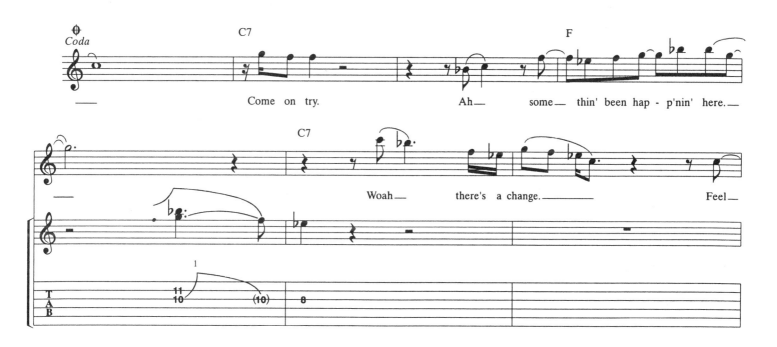

Come on try. Ah— some— thin' been hap-p'nin' here.—

Woah— there's a change.— Feel—

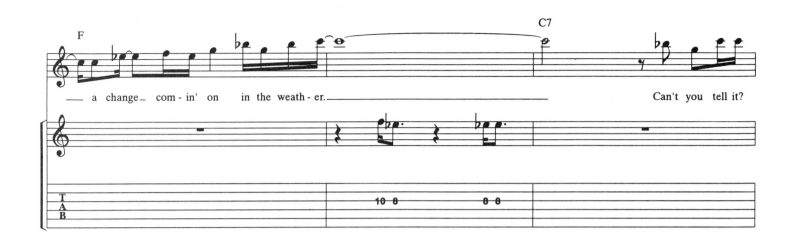

a change com - in' on in the weath - er. Can't you tell it?

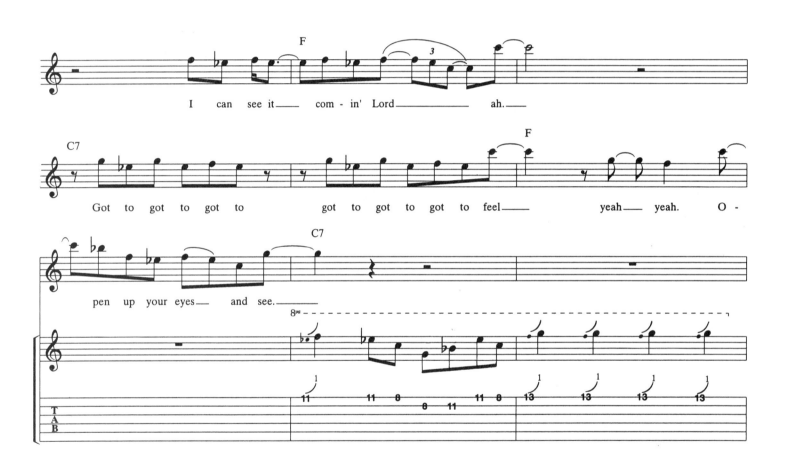

I can see it com - in' Lord ah.

Got to got to got to got to got to got to feel yeah yeah. O -

pen up your eyes and see.

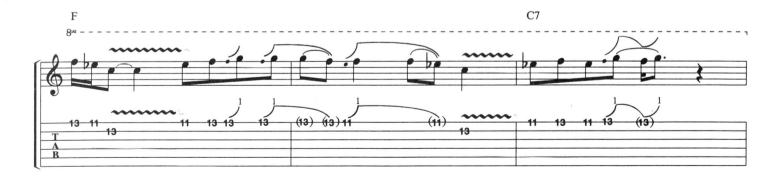

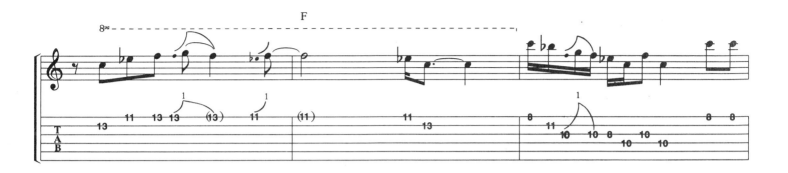

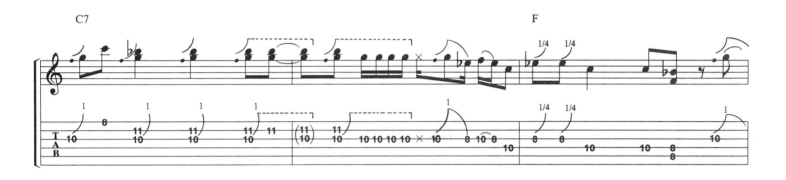

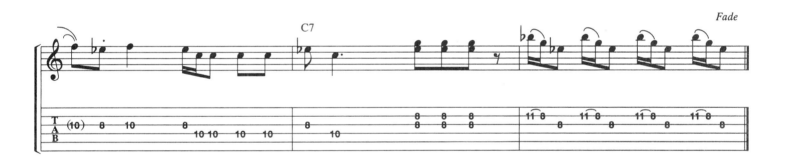

Verse 2 :
You best believe it's true.
The levee's busted, bad news comin' through.
Oh no there ain't no place to hide.
Reach out and pluck you, take you for a ride.
Sheer frustration takin' everything in sight.
Won't be no blastin' if we make it through the night.
Down on your knees for heaven, pray
But every demon got to have his day.
(To Chorus:)

Verse 3 :
High noon I can't believe my eyes.
Wind is ragin' there's a fire in the sky.
Ground shakin' everything comin' loose,
Run like a coward but it ain't no use.
Edge of the river just an ugly scene.
People gettin' pushed, and people gettin' mean.
A change is comin' and gettin' kind of late.
There ain't no survivin', there ain't no escape.
(To Chorus:)

CITIES NEED HELP

By BUDDY GUY

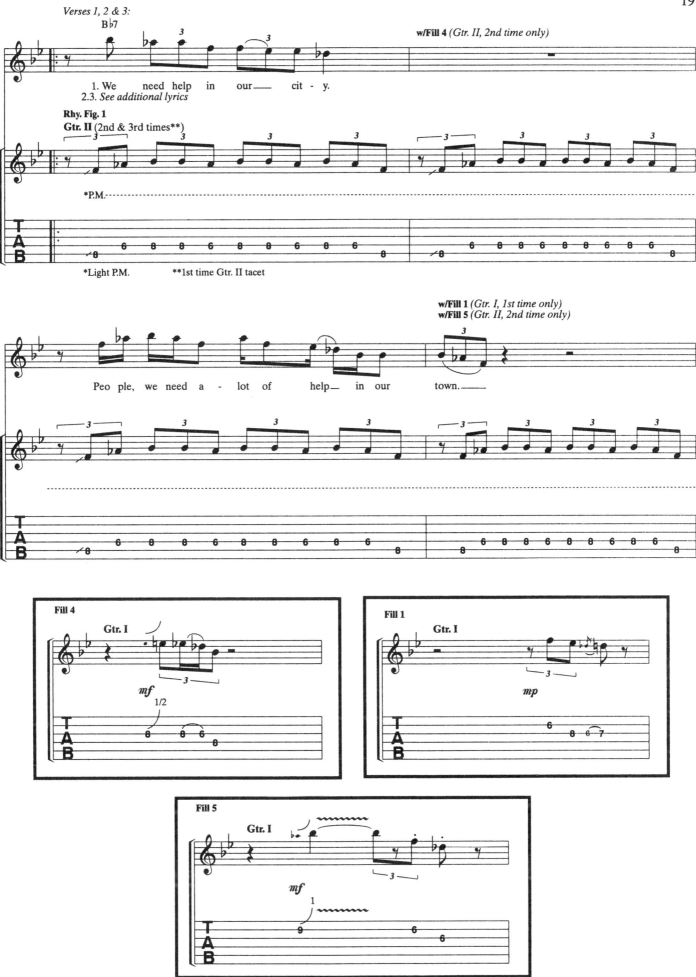

leave 'em a - lone".—

Cities Need Help - 12 - 8

Verse 2:
Weneed help in our school.
We need a lot of help in our home.
We need a lot of help in our school.
We need a lot of help in our home.
But Lord knows somewhere, somehow,
Something gone wrong.

Verse 3:
Thes tried to tear down the highrise,
And the law say that was wrong.
They tried to tear down our highrise,
And the law say that was wrong.
They say, "Long as they killing one another,
You just leave them alone".

COUNTRY MAN

Written by
BUDDY GUY

Moderate shuffle ♩ = 88

Gtr. I
(w/wah)

Verse:

Am7

1. I'm a coun-try man;
2. 3. See additional lyrics.

I was count-ry ev-er since I come to

Gtr. I

Rhy. Fig. 1

Gtr. II mp
(Rhy. gtr.)

*Chord implied.

Country Man - 13 - 1

w/Fill 1 *(2nd time)*
w/Fill 7 *(3rd time)*

town.

Dm7

I'm a coun - try man;_____ I was count - ry when I_____ come to

Country Man - 13 - 2

w/Fill 2 *(2nd time)*
w/Fill 8 *(3rd time)*

town.

You know I can

look at a milk cow____ and I'll

tell you how much her but-ter will____ come a

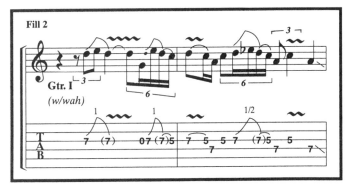

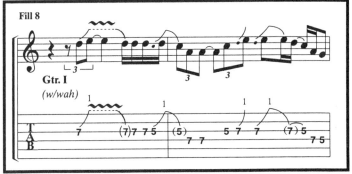

w/Fill 6 *(2nd time)*

Am7

2nd time to Coda I

3rd time to Coda II

have.

Gtr. I *(1st time only)*

Gtr. I *(3rd time only)*

Guitar Solo I

Rhy. Fig. 1 *(2nd time)*

Am7

Gtr. I
(w/wah)

Fill 6

Gtr. I
(w/wah)

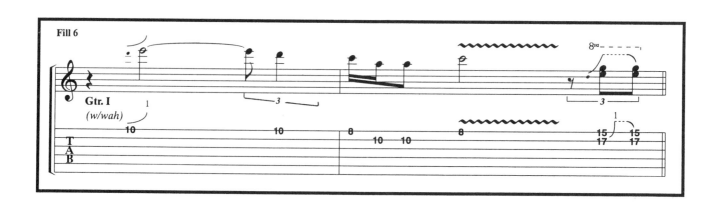

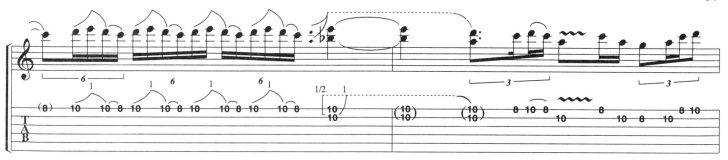

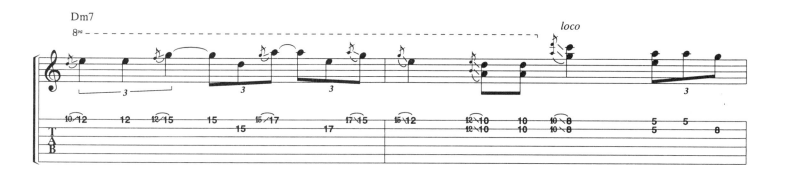

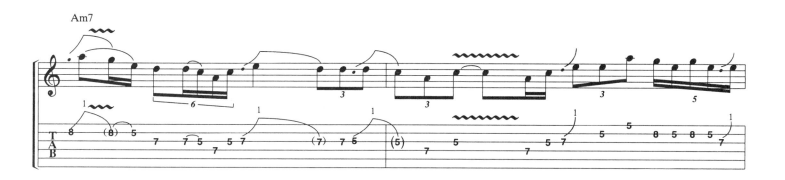

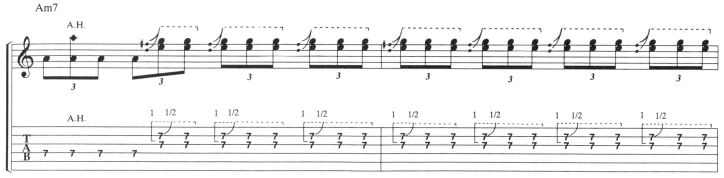

Country Man - 13 - 8

*Steady vibrato while repeating attacks on bent note.

D S. %% al Coda

Am7

Guitar Solo II
w/Rhy. Fig. 1 *(2 times)*

*Vib. bent note only.

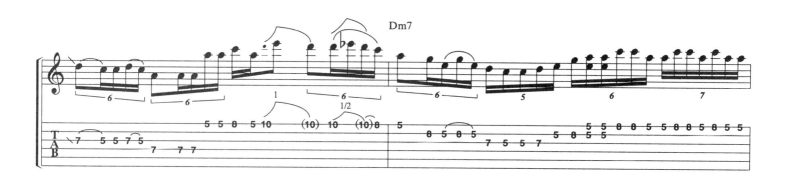

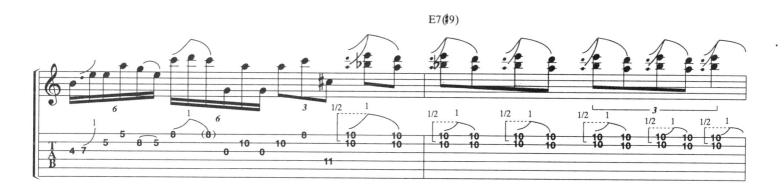

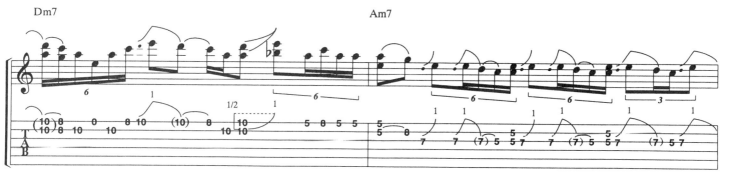

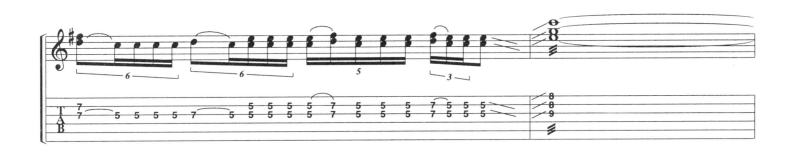

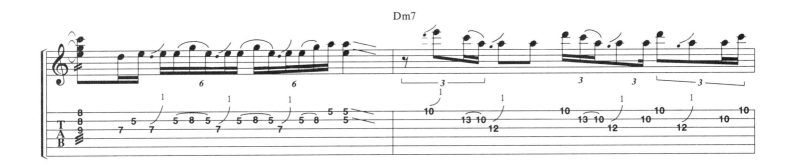

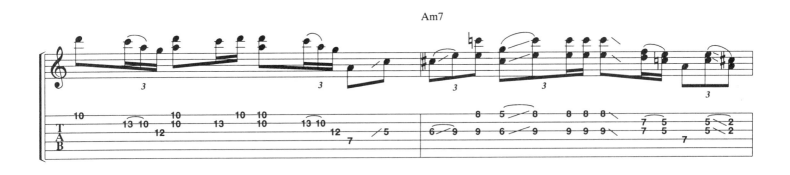

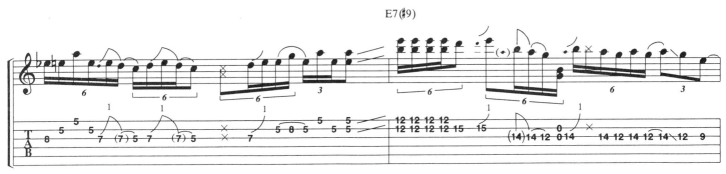

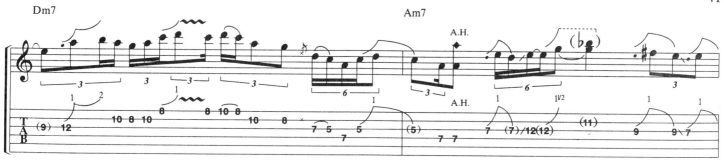

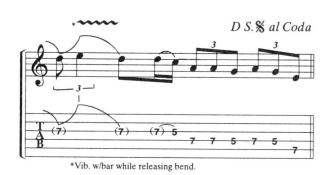

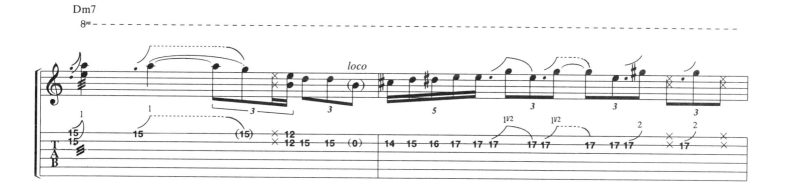

Country Man - 13 - 12

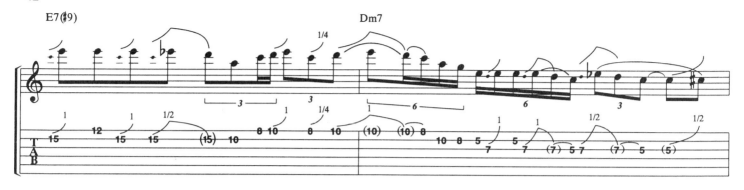

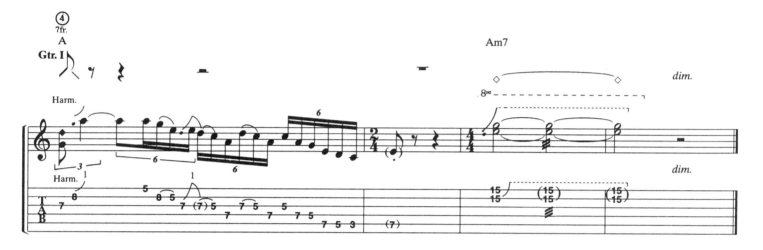

Verse 2:
I'm a country man; just as country as I can be.
I'm a country man; just as country as I can be.
You may get me out of the country, people,
But you never will get the country out of me.
I'm green as a pool table, people, you know I'm twice as square.
Green as a pool table, and you know I'm twice as square.
I wanna be an educated fool, but it's something I don't have.
(To Coda I)

Verse 3:
I'm a country man; I was country when I come to town.
I'm a country man; I was country when I come to town.
You know I can look at a milk cow,
Tell you how much her butter will come a pound.
Just a country man, baby, you know I ain't 'shamed.
I'm a country man, baby, you know I ain't 'shamed.
That's why I'm crazy 'bout my guitar.
That's why I surely will keep on playing.
(To Coda II)

DON'T TELL ME ABOUT THE BLUES

By JAMES "Jamie" QUINN

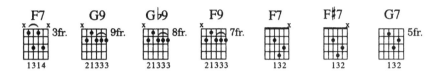

Slow blues ♩. = 67

Intro:
Gtr. I

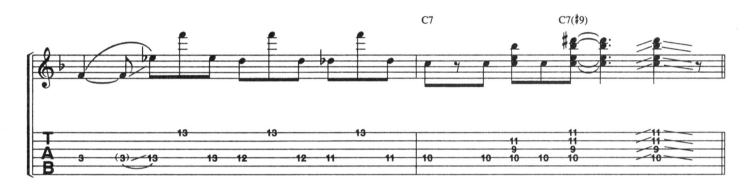

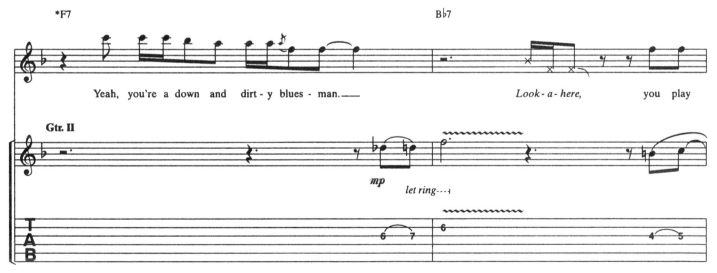

*Chords in plied by acc.

Don't Tell Me About The Blues - 15 - 1

44

blues____ on a blue gui - tar.____

Gtr. I

mf

Gtr. II

let ring------

Ac - cord - ing to the news____ man, as far as____

B7

let ring-------------

F7

____ blues____ goes____ you a star.____

Gtr. I

mf

let ring------------

Don't Tell Me About The Blues - 15 - 3

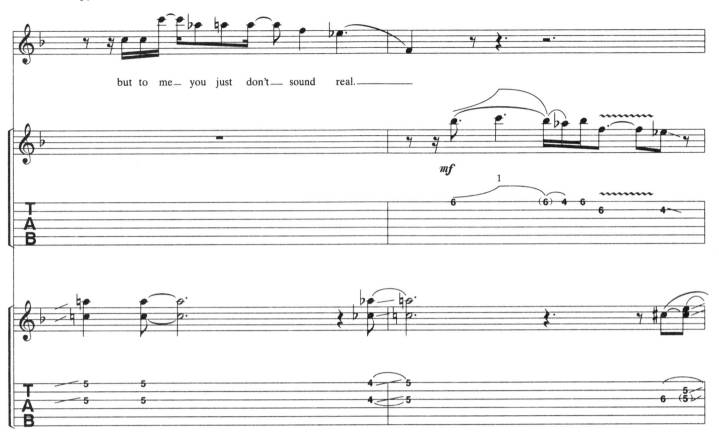

but to me— you just don't— sound real.———

You say you're— down— e - nough— to bor - row.

Gtr. I

Don't Tell Me About The Blues - 15 - 5

please, please, please,——— don't tell me 'bout the Blues.———

Verse 3:
B♭7

4. You tell it like you're bare - foot,——— and you're men

in' those hon - dred dol - lar shoes.———

50

Yeah,— you can shuck and jive— me all you wan - na.— But, please,— please—

don't tell me 'bout— the blues.—

Guitar Solo:
w/Riff A *(Gtr. II, 3 times)*

Don't Tell Me About the Blues - 15 - 9

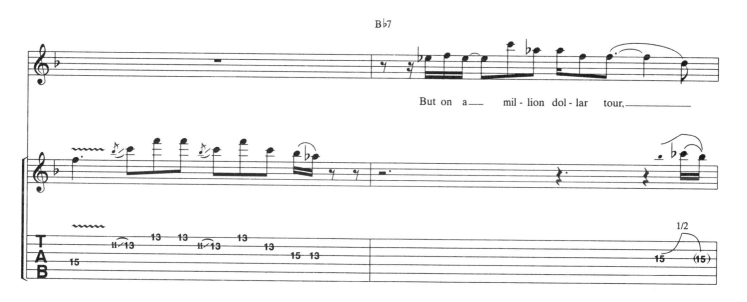

54

man, you can - flash_____ more than a god - damn thing._____

But it's me who's pay - in' my dues._____

So please, man, don't tell___ me a - bout the blues._____

Guitar solo:
w/Rhy. Fig. 1 *(Gtr. II) simile*

Don't Tell Me About the Blues - 15 - 12

*Tremolo pick while trilling.

*Tremolo pick while trilling.

Don't Tell Me About the Blues - 15 - 15

DAMN RIGHT, I'VE GOT THE BLUES

By BUDDY GUY

Damn Right, I've Got the Blues – 8 – 1

Damn Right, I've Got the Blues – 8 – 2

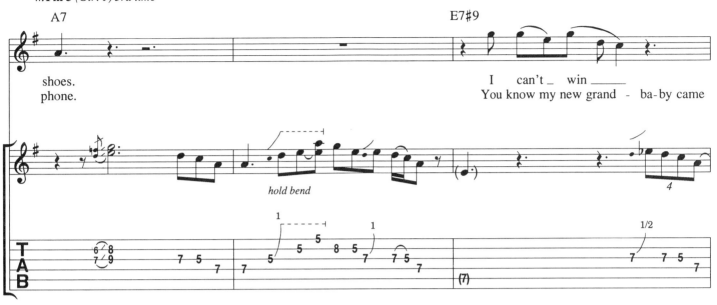

w/Fill 4 *(Gtr. 1) 2nd time*
w/Fill 6 *(Gtr. 1) 3rd time*

'cause I don't have a   thing _ to lose.
to the door and said,   "Grand - dad - dy,   you know ain't no one at home."

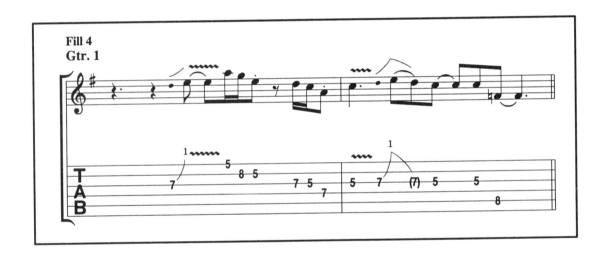

Guitar Solo:

w/Rhy. Fig. 1 *(Gtr. 2) simile*

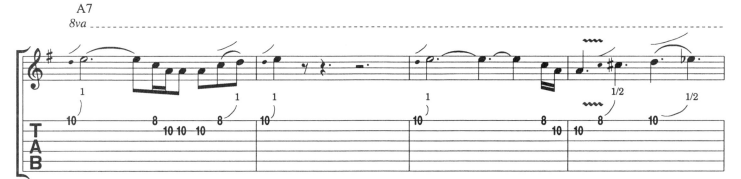

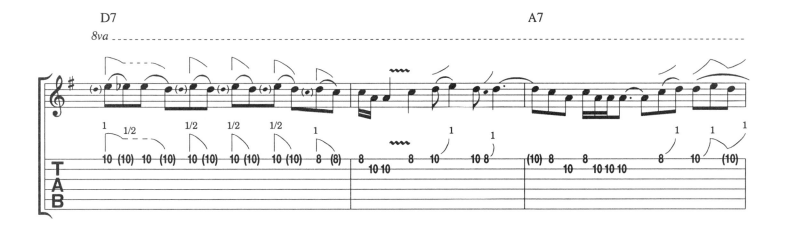

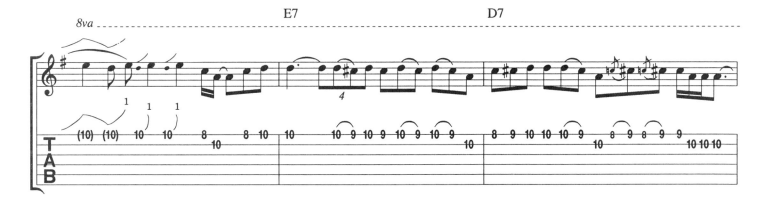

D.S. % al Coda

You're

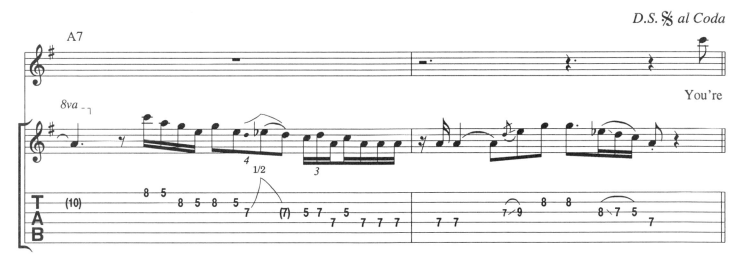

Damn Right, I've Got the Blues – 8 – 6

Coda

w/Fill 7 *(Gtr. 2) 2 times*

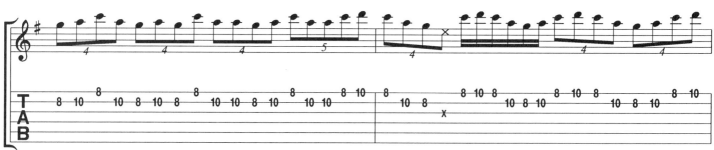

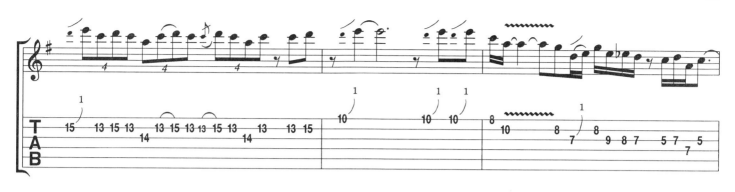

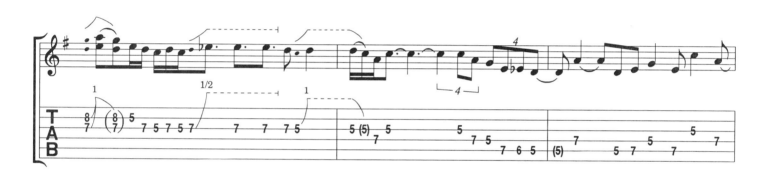

Gtrs. 1 & 2

3 times

w/Fill 7 *(Gtr. 2) to end*

*8 times and fade

You're damn _ right   I've got the blues. _

Gtr. 1

Damn Right, I've Got the Blues – 8 – 8

**Gtrs. 1 & 2 continue
in unison 5th time.*

FEELS LIKE RAIN

Written by
JOHN HIATT

Moderately ♩ = 75

Intro:

Verse:

1. Down here the riv-er_____ leads to sea.

And in this stick-y heat I feel you

Feels Like Rain - 12 - 1

Feels Like Rain - 12 - 2

Feels Like Rain - 12 - 6

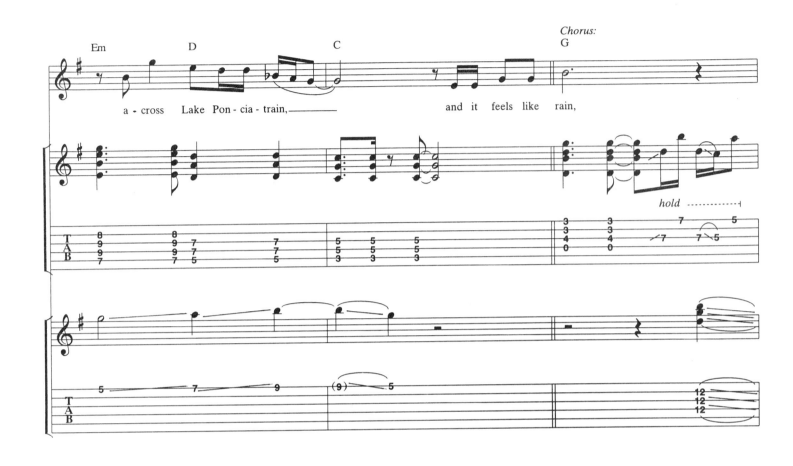

Verse:

So but-ton down the hatch ba - by,—

and leave - your heart up your sleeve.—

It looks like we're in for storm - y weath - er.—

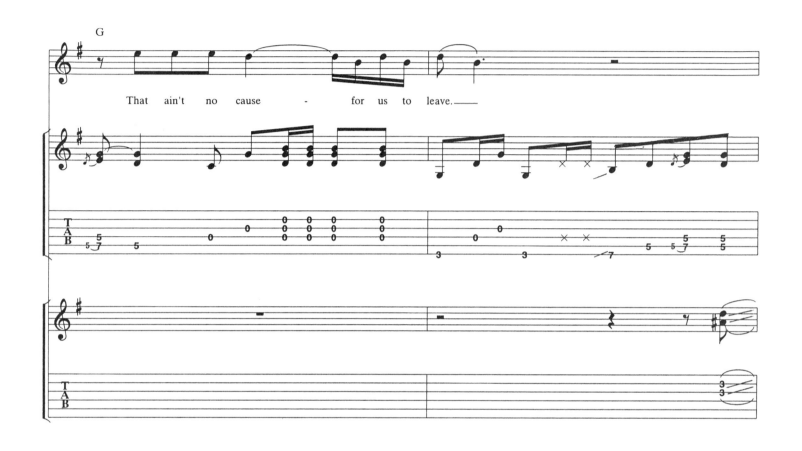

That ain't no cause - for us to leave.

Just lie here ___ in my arms. ___ Let it wash a - way the

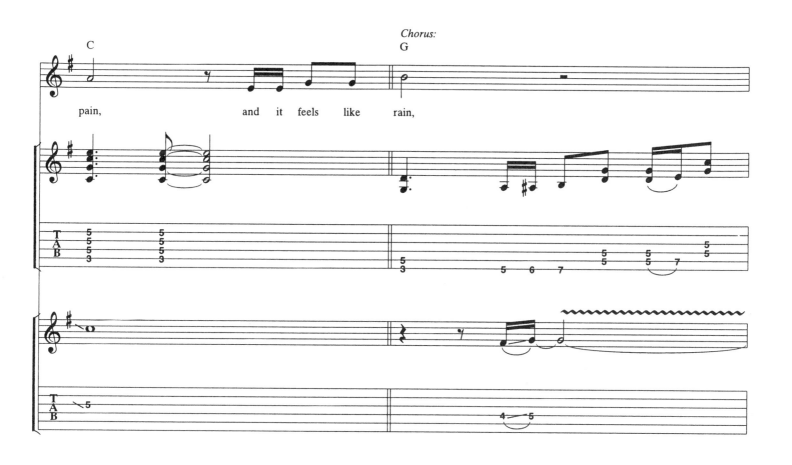

Chorus:

pain,   and   it   feels   like   rain,

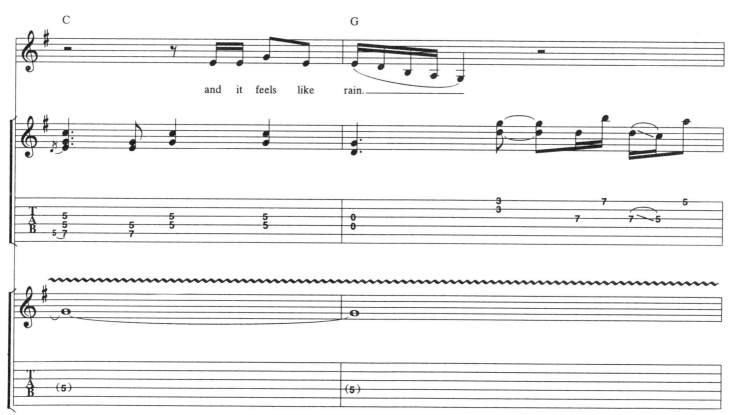

and   it   feels   like   rain._____

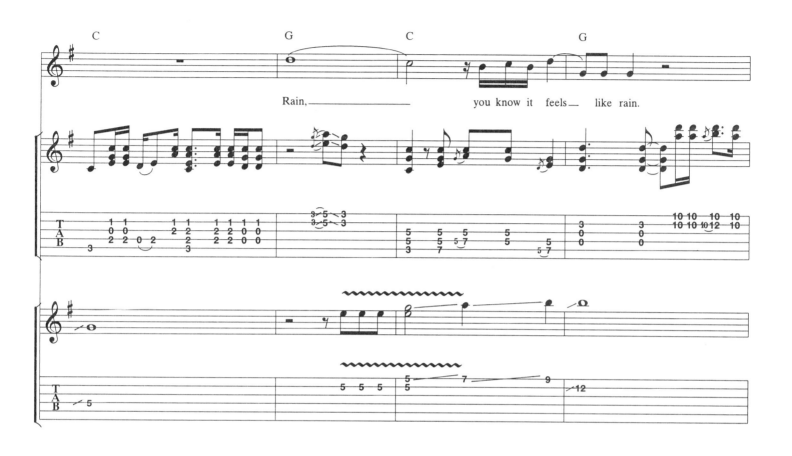

Rain,_____ you know it feels__ like rain.

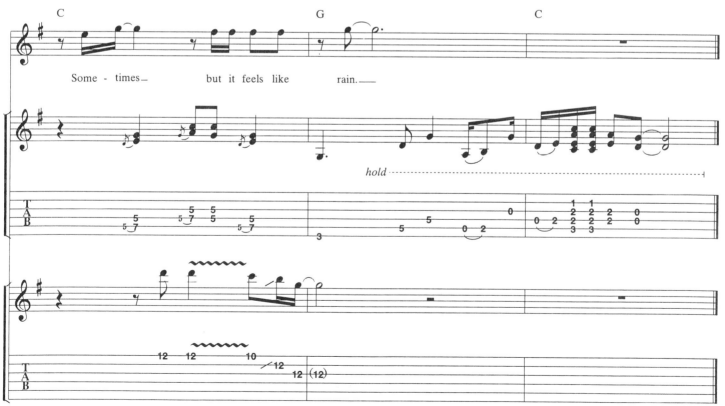

Some - times__ but it feels like rain.__

LET ME LOVE YOU BABY

Words and Music by
WILLIE DIXON

*Gradually release bend.

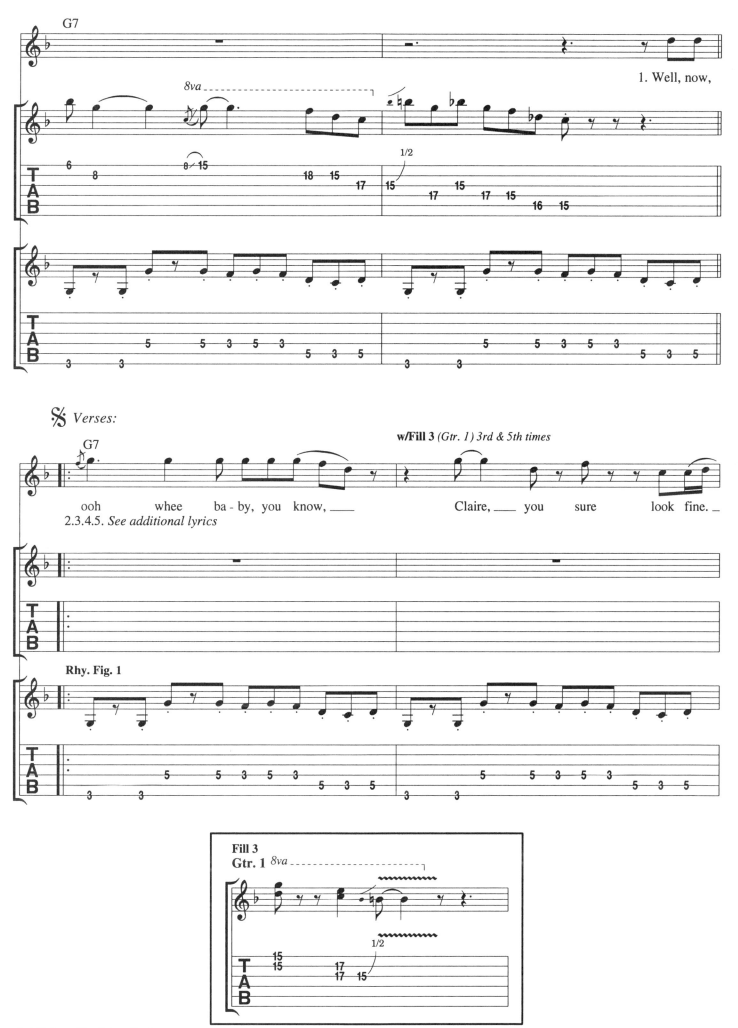

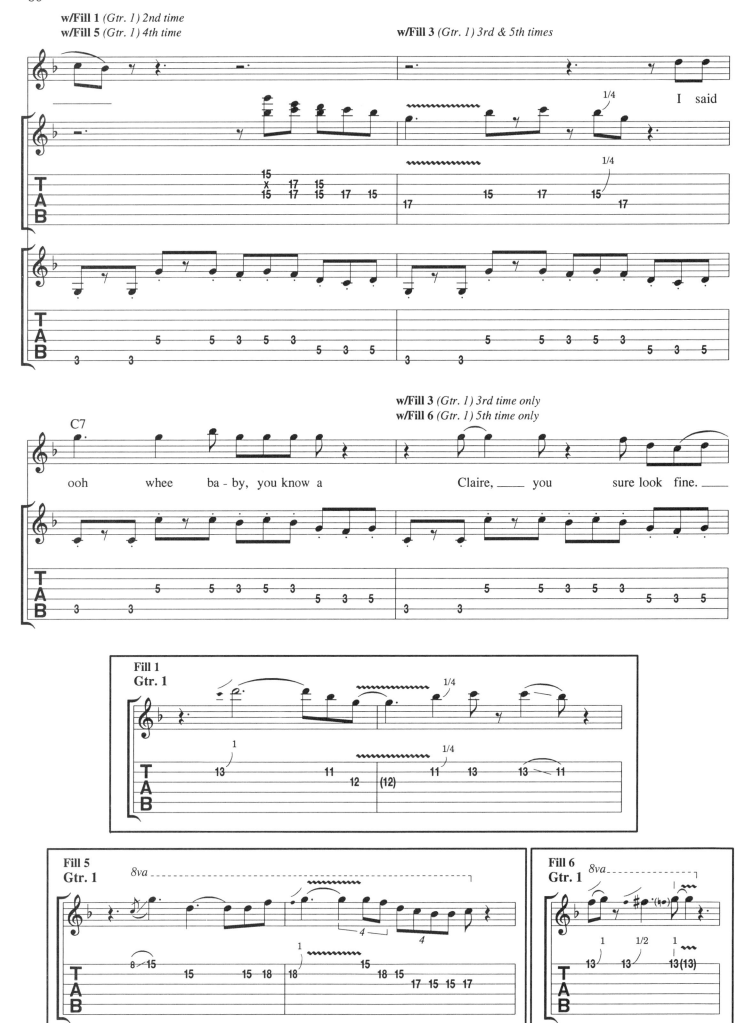

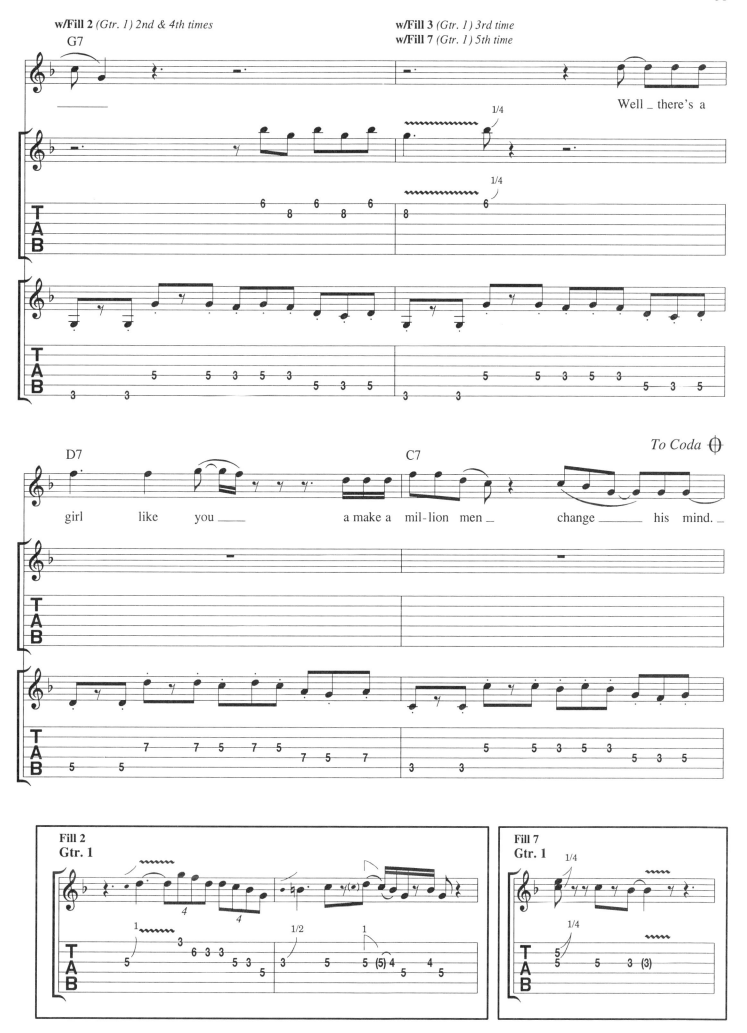

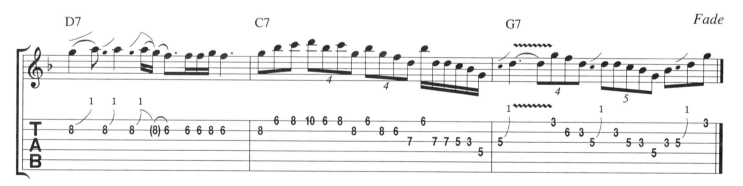

Verse 2:
Baby, when you walk you know you shake like a willow tree.
I say, baby, when you walk, woman, you know you shake like a willow tree.
Why does a girl like you love to make a fool of me.

Verses 3 & 5:
Let me love you, baby. Let me love you, baby.
Let me love you, baby. Let me love you, baby.
Let me love you, baby 'til your good love drive me crazy.

Verse 4:
Well now, baby, when you walk you know you shake like a willow tree.
Yah baby, when you walk, woman, you know you shake just like a willow tree.
Babe, a woman like you, ah would love to make a fool of me.

LITTLE DAB-A-DOO

By BUDDY GUY

Little Dab-a-Doo - 12 - 1

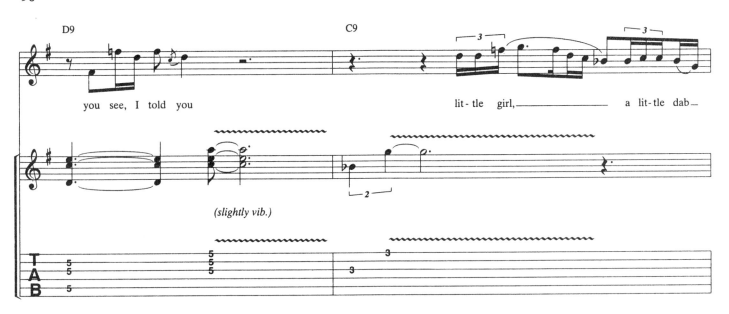

you see, I told you   lit-tle girl,_____ a lit-tle dab—

(slightly vib.)

will do.—

(Spoken:) let me hear it...

grad. bend

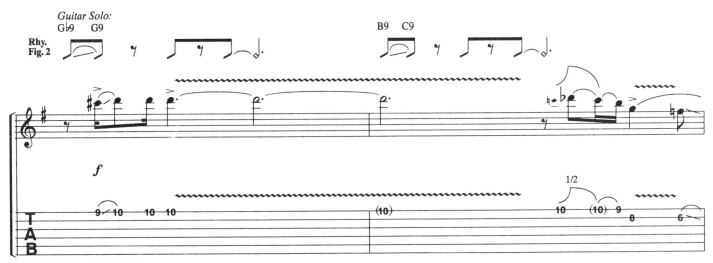

Guitar Solo:

Rhy. Fig. 2

Little Dab-a-Doo - 12 - 6

an' I told__ you_____ a lit-tle dab__ will do._____

ya - ba - da - ba - do!

Little Dab-a-Doo - 12 - 11

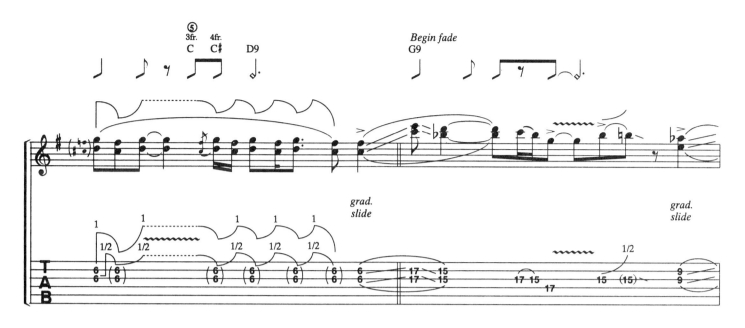

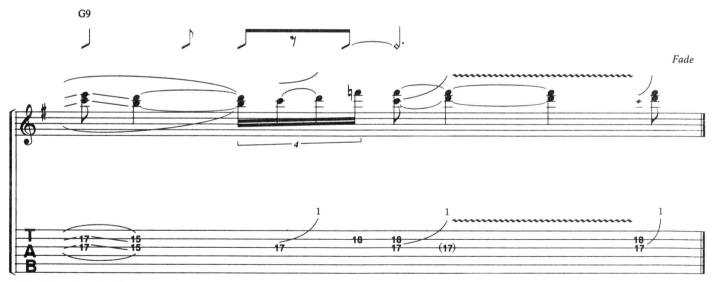

Little Dab-a-Doo - 12 - 12

PLEASE DON'T DRIVE ME AWAY

By CHARLES BROWN and JESSE ERVIN

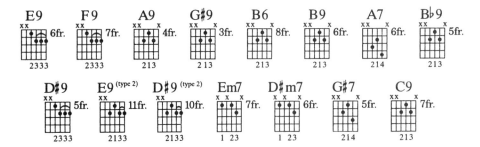

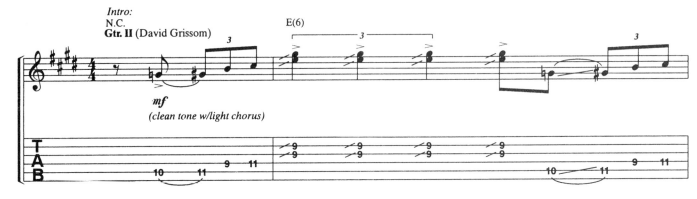

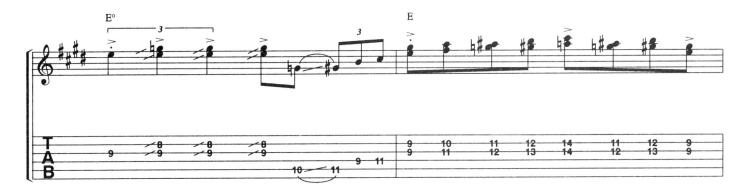

Please Don't Drive Me Away - 14 - 1

Please Don't Drive Me Away - 14 - 4

don't you drive_____ me a - way,_____ no._____

*Play "behind the beat" slightly.

*Duplicates pitches two octaves lower than played; transcription reflects pitches as played on the guitar (as opposed to the "sounding" pitches, created by the octave pedal).

106

Please Don't Drive Me Away - 14 - 9

Please Don't Drive Me Away - 14 - 10

108

Please Don't Drive Me Away - 14 - 11

Please Don't Drive Me Away - 14 - 12

Please Don't Drive Me Away - 14 - 13

Please Don't Drive Me Away - 14 - 14

REMEMBERIN' STEVIE

By BUDDY GUY

*Gtr. 2 is an approximate combination of the 2 rhythm gtr. parts

*As B♭ to C bend is held with 3rd finger, 4th finger plays the D♭ and releases.

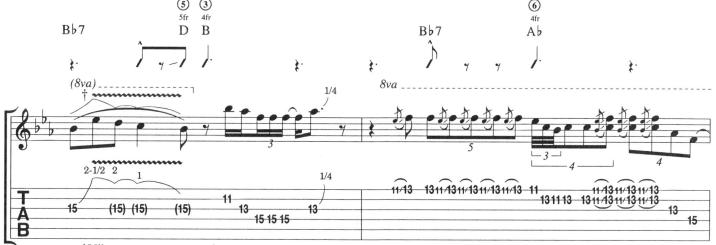

†Vibrato occurs at top of 2nd note.

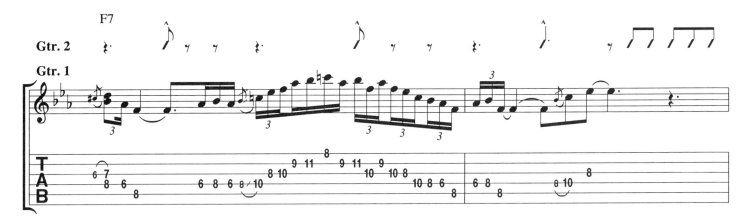

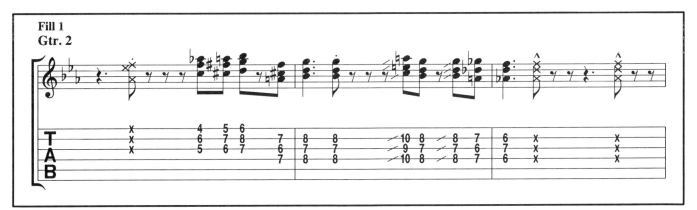

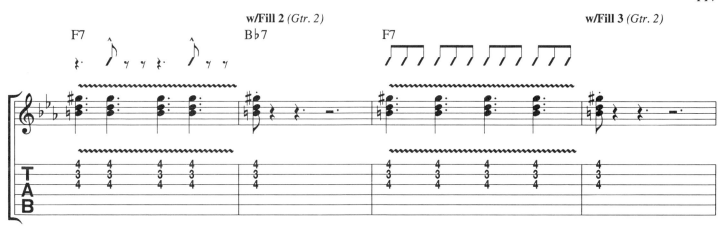

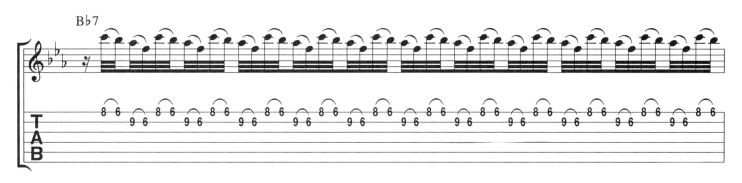

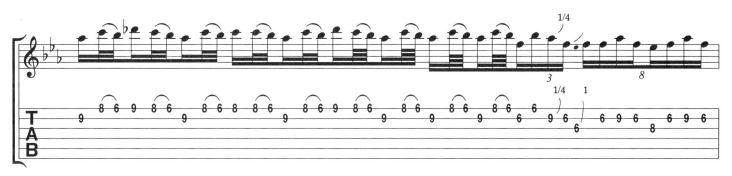

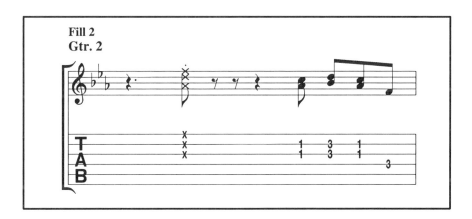

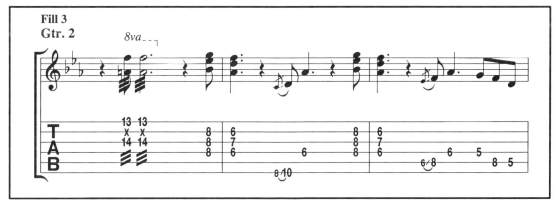

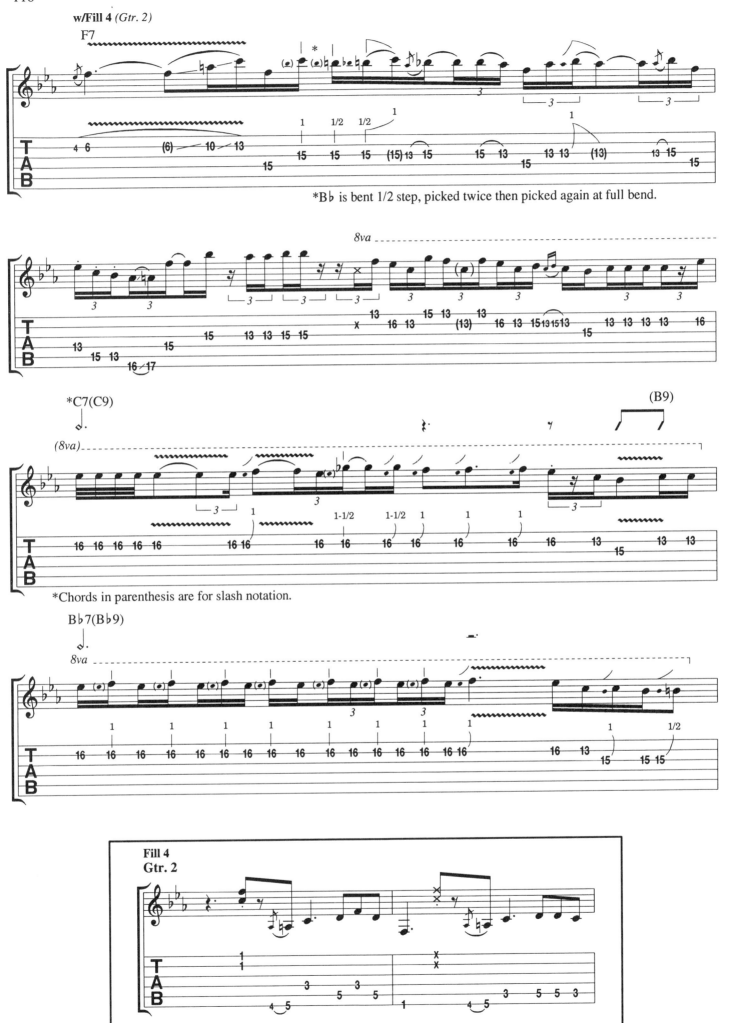

*Bb is bent 1/2 step, picked twice then picked again at full bend.

*Chords in parenthesis are for slash notation.

*Bend 17 up 1 1/2 steps, hold bend and pull off to the 15th fret.

w/Fill 5 *(Gtr. 2)*

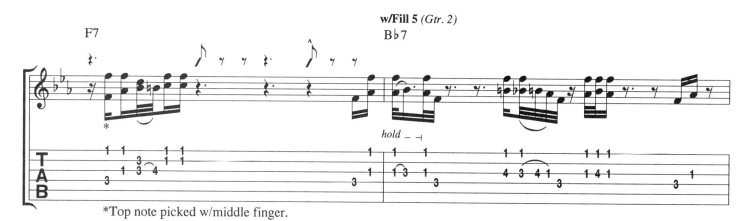

*Top note picked w/middle finger.

w/Fill 6 *(Gtr. 2)*

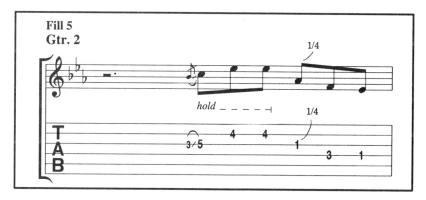

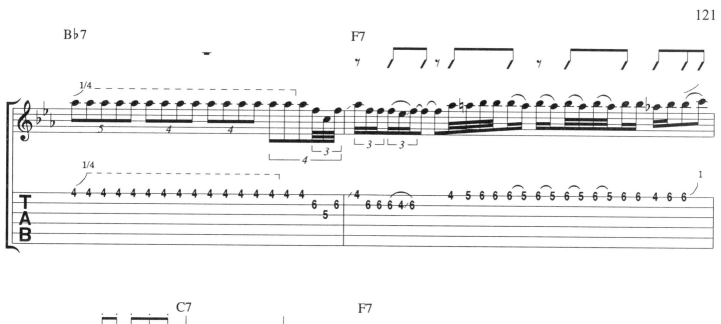

Rememberin' Stevie – 14 – 10

*String noise.

124

Rememberin' Stevie – 14 – 13

SHE'S A SUPERSTAR

**Written by
BUDDY GUY**

She's A Superstar - 14 - 1

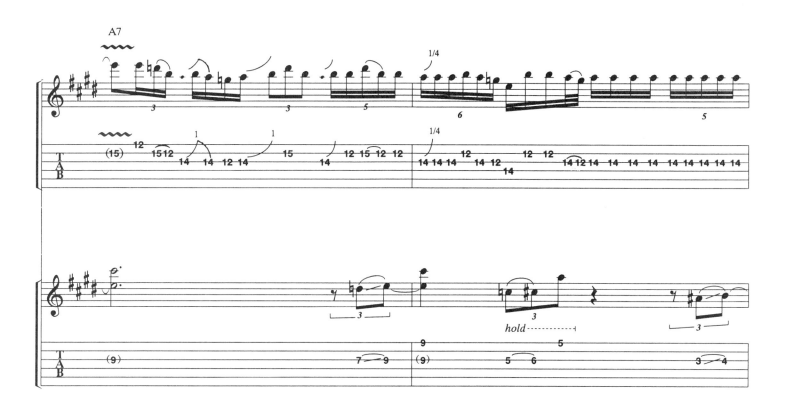

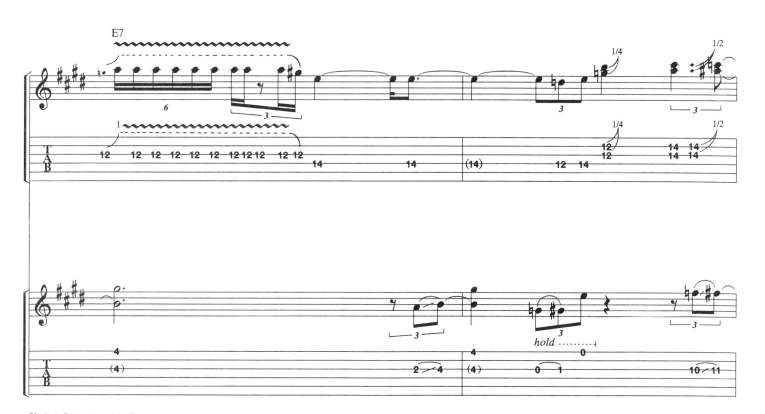

She's A Superstar - 14 - 2

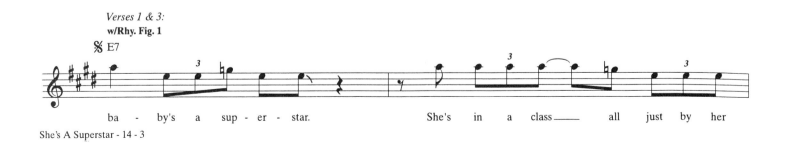

ba - by's a sup - er - star.   She's in a class____ all just by her

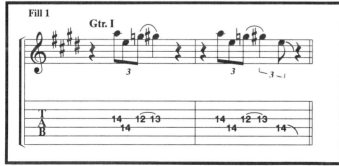

She's A Superstar - 14 - 4

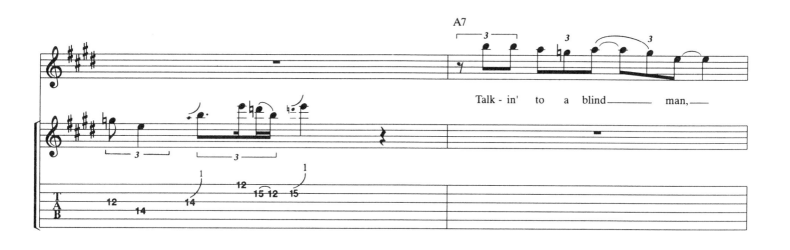

Talk - in' to a blind_____ man,_____

talk - in' to a blind_____ man the o - ther night._____

He said "ev-'ry wom - an you talk - in' a - bout, "bud", he said

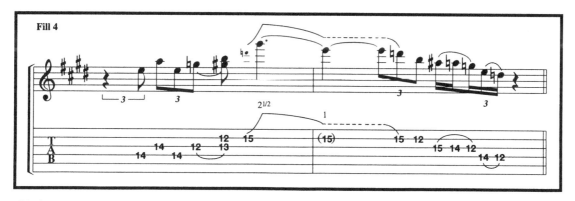

Fill 4

132

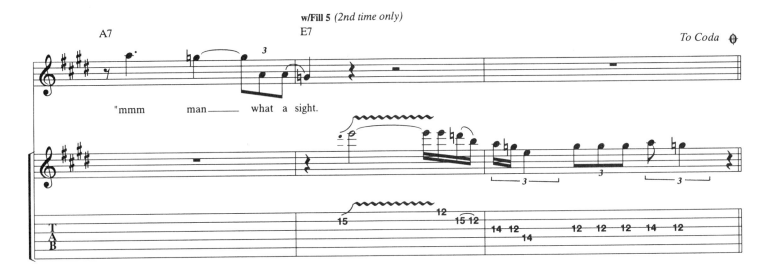

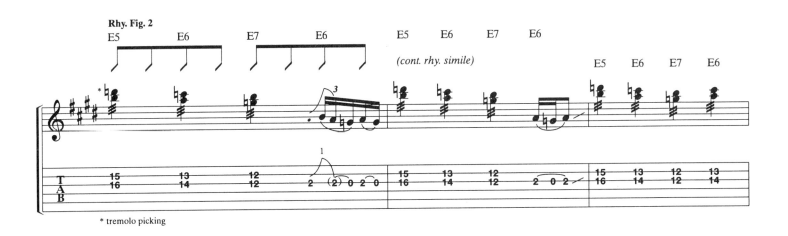

* tremolo picking

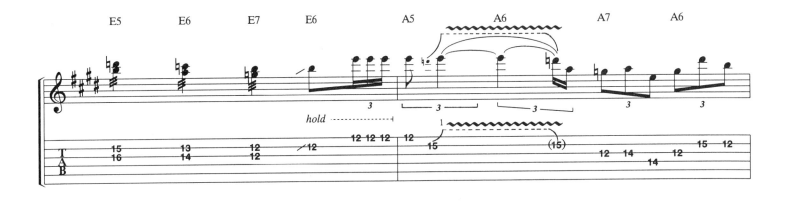

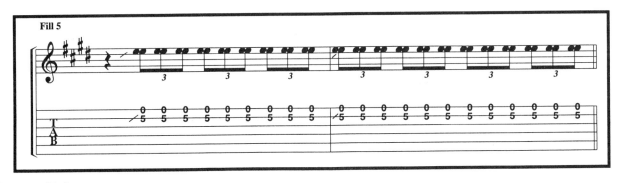

She's A Superstar - 14 - 7

She say's she should be on cen-ter fold— of the

Play - boy——— mag - a - zine.

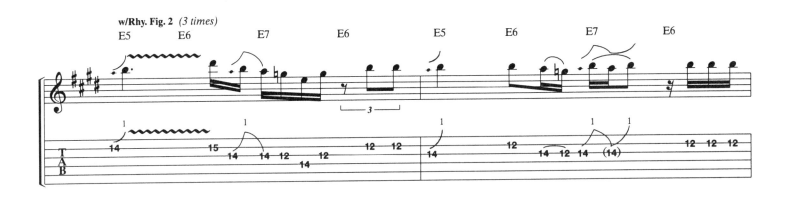

w/Rhy. Fig. 2 *(3 times)*

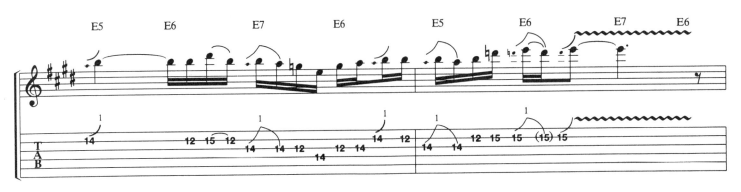

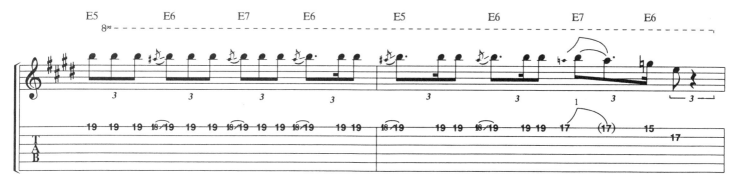

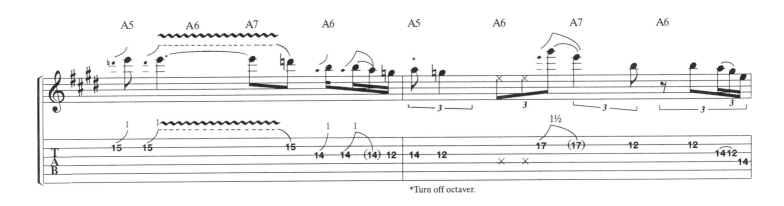

*Turn off octaver.

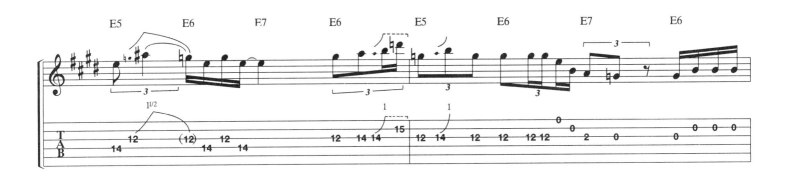

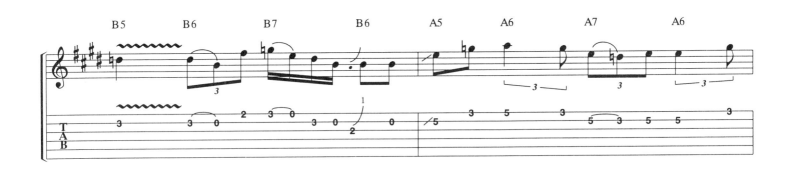

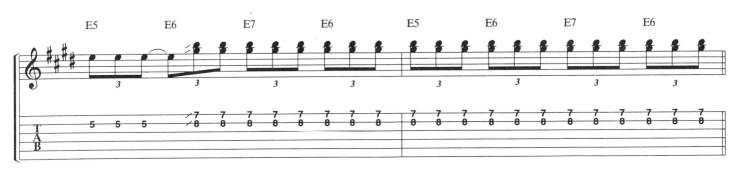

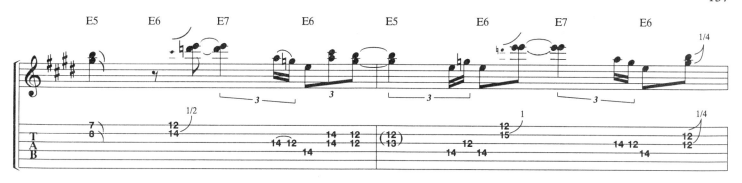

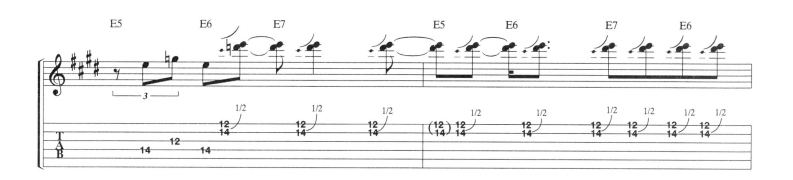

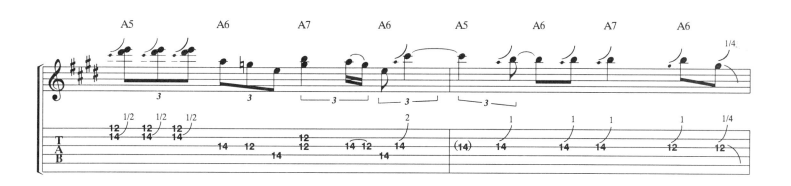

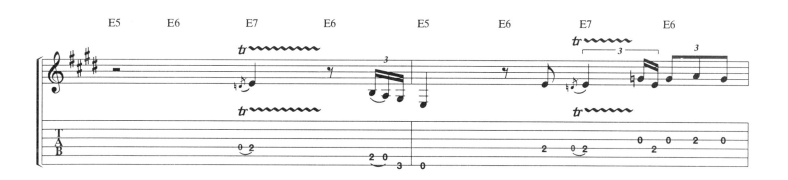

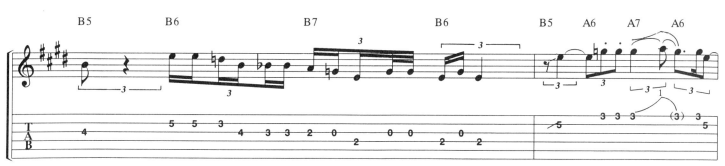

She's A Superstar - 14 - 12

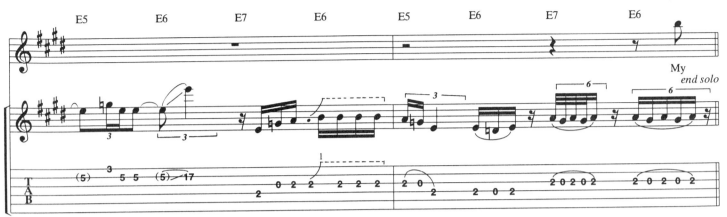

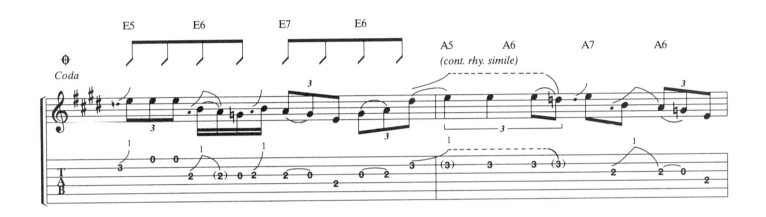

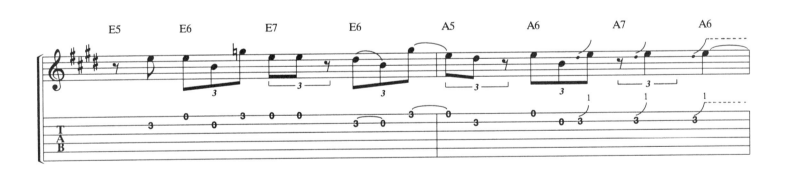

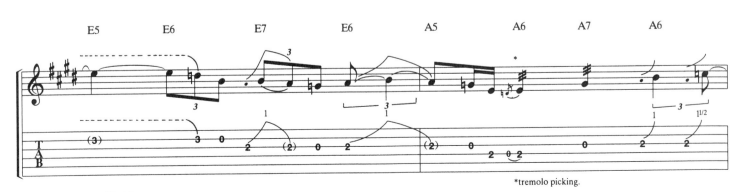

She's A Superstar - 14 - 13

*tremolo picking.

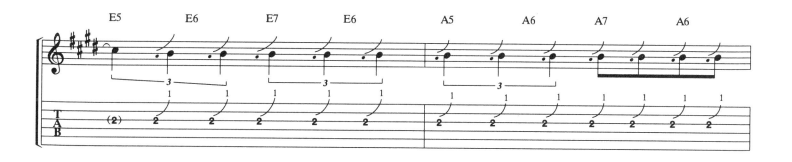

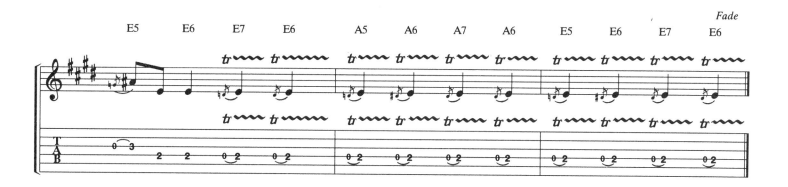

Verse 4:
My baby's a superstar,
And I love her like I do my guitar.
My baby's a superstar,
And I love her like I do my guitar.
I don't care what they say about another
 woman,
I don't care who she are.
(To Coda)

SHE'S NINETEEN YEARS OLD

Written by
MUDDY WATERS

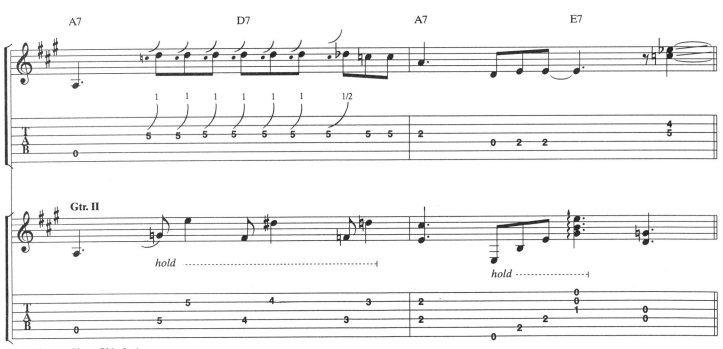

She's Nineteen Years Old - 8 - 1

Verses 1 & 3:

1. 3.I'm say'n some - thing to you.___ I don't care_ how you feel.

Rhy. Fig. 1

You just don't re - al - ize you got your - self a good deal.

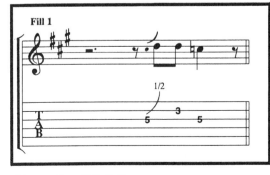

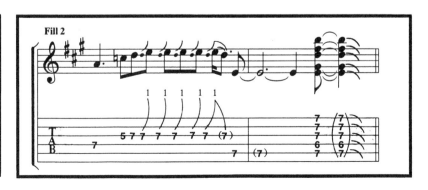

She's nine-teen years old   and she got   ways___ just like a ba-by child.

She's Nineteen Years Old - 8 - 3

Noth - ing I can do to please her.

I'm just try'n to make this lit - tle wom - an feel___ sat - is -

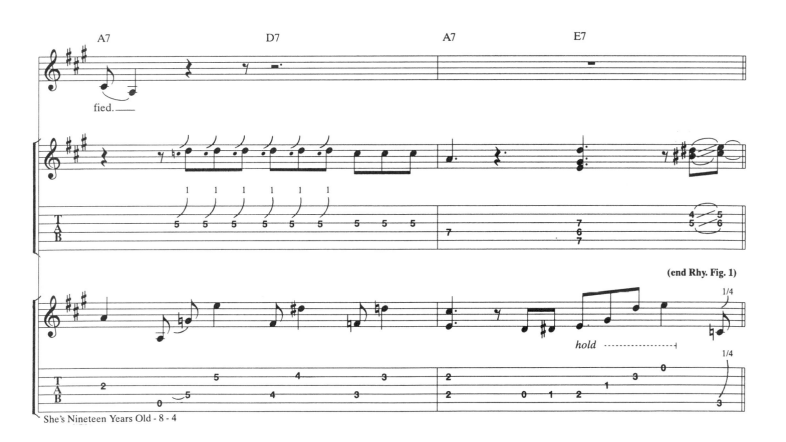

fied.___

(end Rhy. Fig. 1)

hold - - - - - - - - - - - - - - - -

144

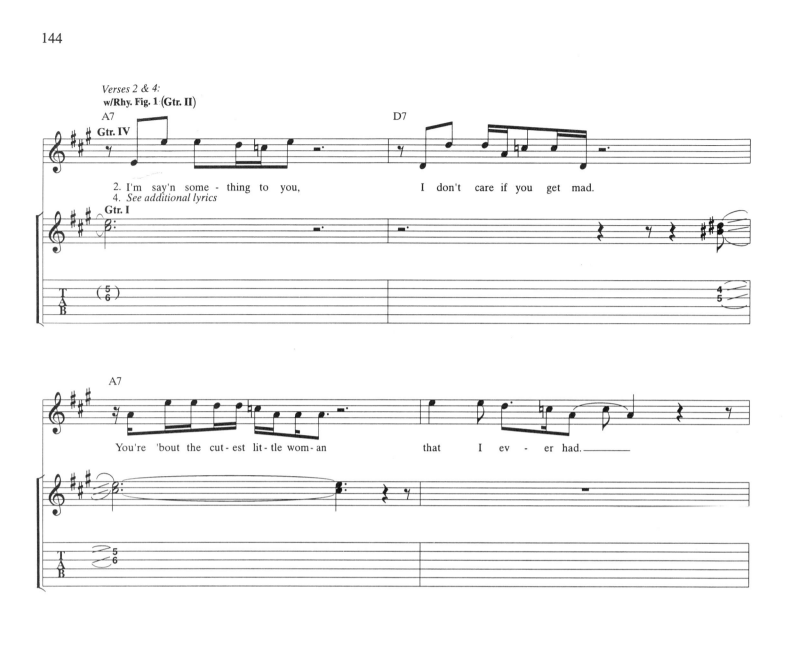

She's Nineteen Years Old - 8 - 5

She's Nineteen Years Old - 8 - 6

Verse 4:
I can't ask her where she's going.
She tells me where she's been.
She'll start a conversation
That don't have no end.
She's nineteen years old,
She's got ways just like a baby child.
Nothing I can do to please her...
(To Coda)

TROUBLE BLUES

By CHARLES BROWN

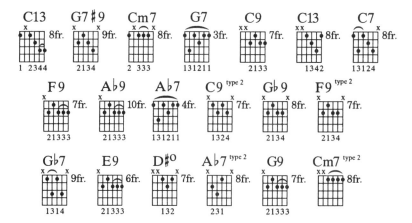

Slow blues ♩. = 53

Trouble Blues - 4 - 1

150

Trouble Blues - 4 - 3

Verse 2:
Trouble, trouble and this misery
You're about to get
the best of me
Someday darlin' someday darlin'
I won't be trouble no more

Verse 3:
I told you my story
I've sung my song
about you leavin'
you know that's wrong
bye bye darlin' bye bye darlin'
I won't be trouble no more

Trouble Blues - 4 - 4

TOO BROKE TO SPEND THE NIGHT

By BUDDY GUY

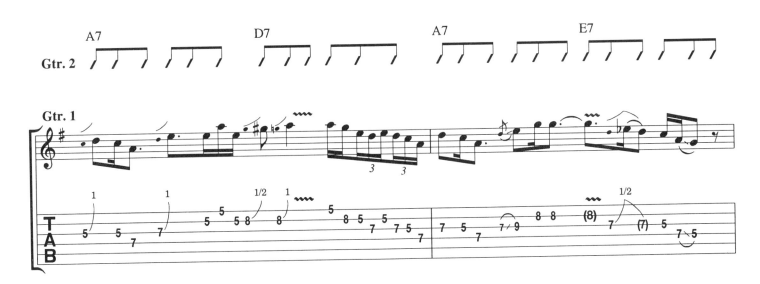

Too Broke to Spend the Night – 9 – 1

w/Fill 2 *(Gtr. 1) 2nd time only*
w/Fill 6 *(Gtr. 1) 3rd time only*
w/Fill 11 *(Gtr. 1) 4th time only*

I know it ain't right.

am.
ring.

I said my
I said, yah I

Fill 2
Gtr. 1

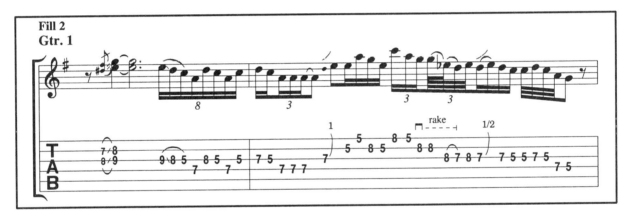

Fill 6
Gtr. 1

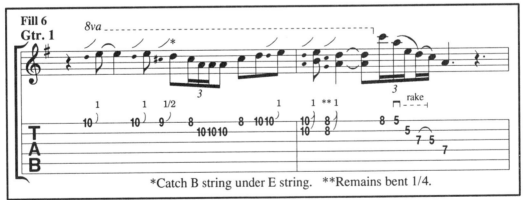

*Catch B string under E string.   **Remains bent 1/4.

Fill 11
Gtr. 1

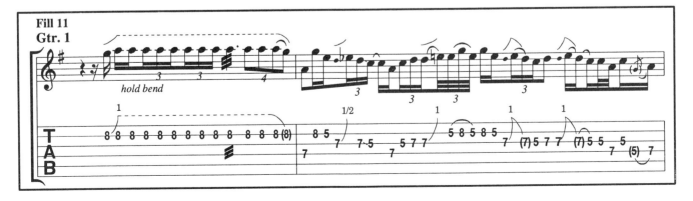

hold bend

I'm catch-ing hell__ out here__ and peo-ple you know I know it ain't

on - ly son, _____ I don't think, I don't think he real-ly know who I

pawned my watch, _____ ba - by, you know I pawned my dog-gone ring.

Fill 7
Gtr. 1

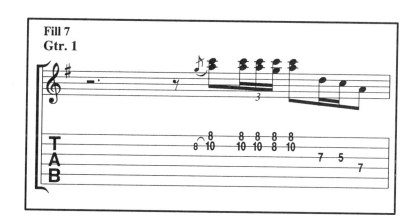

Fill 12
Gtr. 1

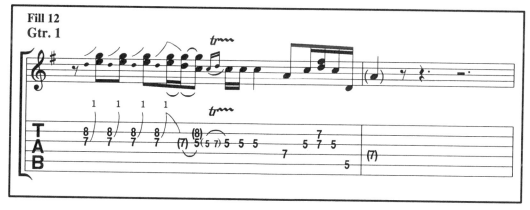

w/Fill 8 *(Gtr. 1) 3rd time only*   **w/Fill 13** *(Gtr. 1) 4th time only*

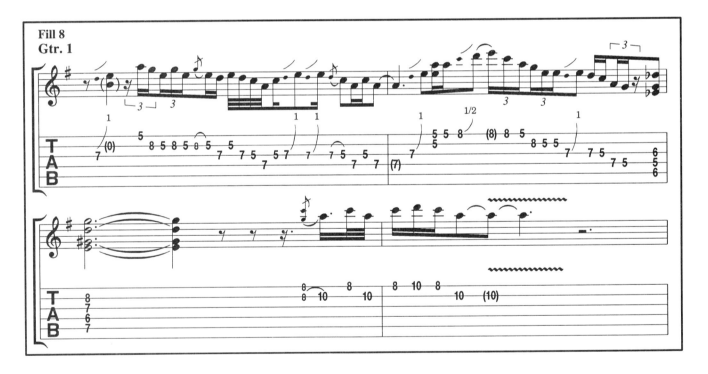

w/**Fill 3** *(Gtr. 1) 2nd time only*

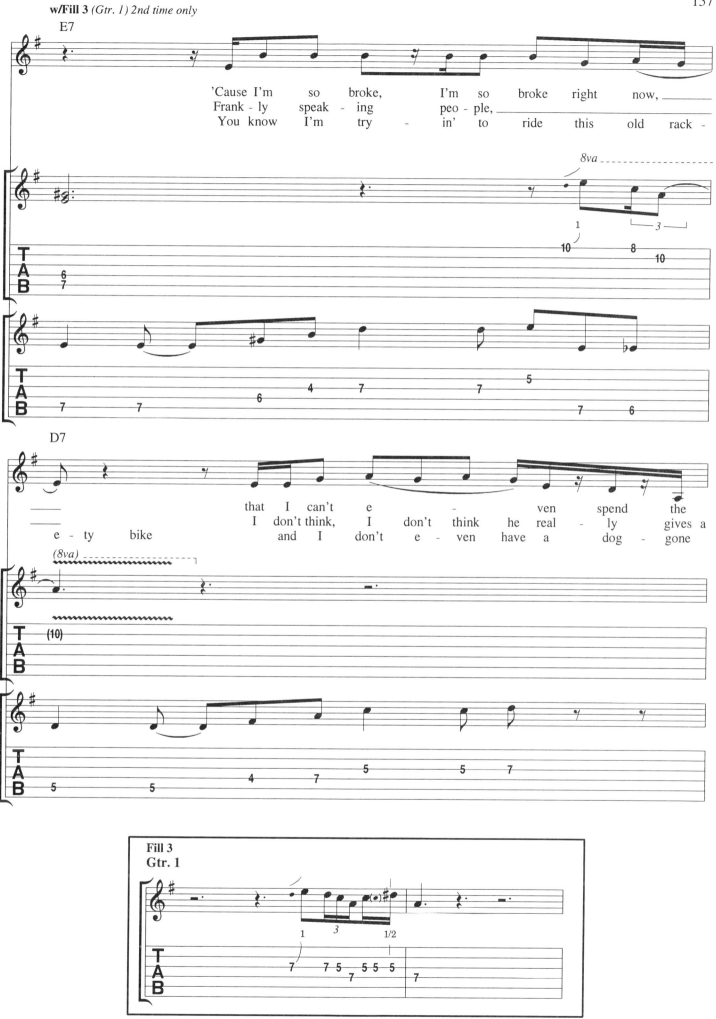

'Cause I'm so broke, I'm so broke right now, _____
Frank - ly speak - ing peo - ple, _____
You know I'm try - in' to ride this old rack -

that I can't e - ven spend the
I don't think, I don't think he real - ly gives a
e - ty bike and I don't e - ven have a dog - gone

Fill 3
Gtr. 1

Guitar Solo: